KiM'S PLACE

and other poems
by

LEE BENNETT HOPKINS

drawings by   Di FioRi

80339
June, 1974
Holt, Rinehart and Winston
New York · Chicago · San Francisco

Hopkins, Lee Bennett.
   Kim's place.

   SUMMARY: Sixteen poems reflecting the life of
the very young and attitudes about such things as
rain, color, puppies, dreams, mirrors, and fear.
   Poems.
   1. Children's poetry. [1. American poetry]
I. Di Fiori, Lawrence, illus. II. Title.
PZ8.3.H776Ki   811'.5'4   73-14613
ISBN 0-03-012081-0

"I'm Not Afraid" and "Some Rainy Days" originally appeared in
Humpty Dumpty's Magazine

   Printed in the United States of America
   Designed by Lawrence Di Fiori
   First Edition

To Miriam Chaikin ....
        because ....
            L. B. H.

KIM'S PLACE

This is my room
My very own place.

This is my mirror
There is my face.

These are my books.
I have over 30.

This is my baseball
And my rag-doll called Gertie.

This is my place
Do you know how I know?

There's a sign on the wall
That tells me it's so.

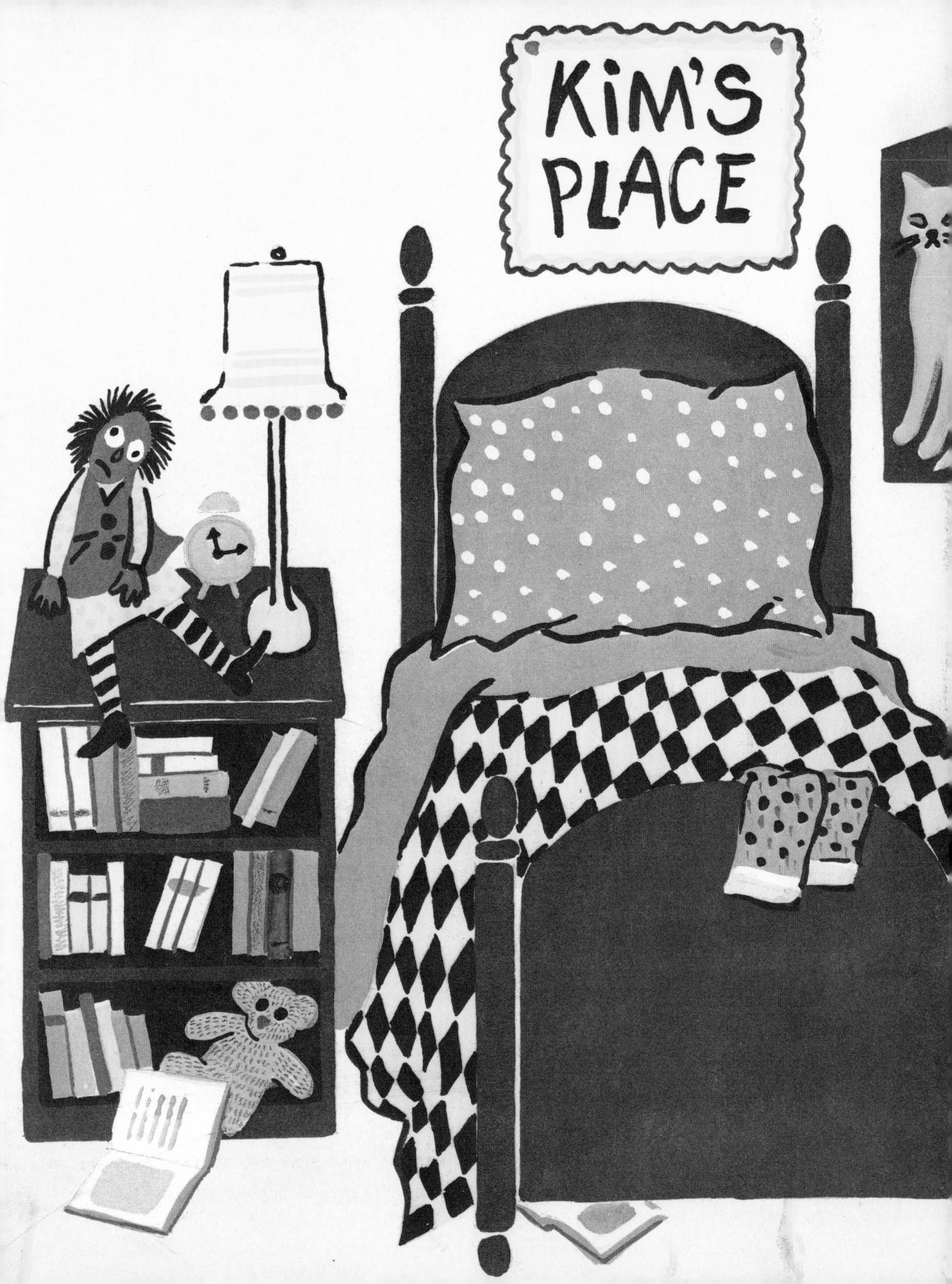
KIM'S
PLACE

For Mother

Happy
Birthday

KiM

MY NAME

I wrote my name on the sidewalk
But the rain washed it away.

I wrote my name on my hand
But the soap washed it away.

I wrote my name on the birthday card
I gave to Mother today

And there it will stay
For mother never throws

ANYTHING

of mine away!

COMPANY

My face is dirty
My blouse is torn
My slacks are baggy
My shoes are worn.

Grandma's coming.

Watch Mother hide me
—as if my wrapping's more important
than what I feel inside me!

QUESTION

If cookies come in boxes
      And tuna comes in cans
And the butcher bakes our roast beef
      And wraps it in Saran

If most cakes come from bakeries
      And doughnuts from the store
I often sit and wonder
      What our kitchen oven's for?

GIRLS CAN, TOO!

Tony said: "Boys are better!

    They can . . .
        whack a ball,
        ride a bike with one hand
        leap off a wall."

I just listened
and when he was through,
I laughed and said:

    "Oh, yeah! Well, girls can, too!"

Then I leaped off the wall
    and rode away
With *his* 200 baseball cards

    I won that day.

LAST LAUGH

They all laughed when I told them
I wanted to be

A woman in space
Floating so free.

But they won't laugh at me
When they finally see
My feet up on Mars
And my face on TV.

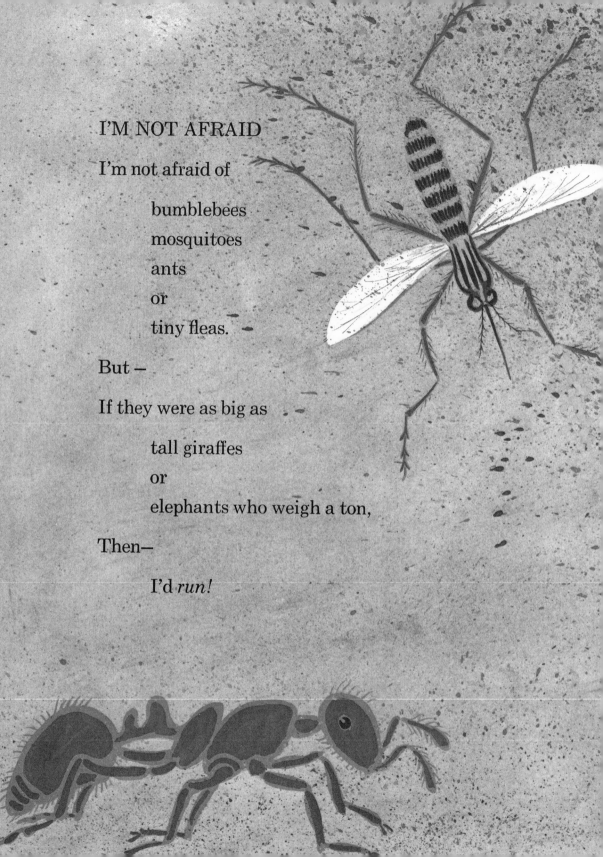

I'M NOT AFRAID

I'm not afraid of

      bumblebees
      mosquitoes
      ants
      or
      tiny fleas.

But —

If they were as big as

      tall giraffes
      or
      elephants who weigh a ton,

Then—

      I'd *run!*

RAINY DAYS

Some rainy days I go outside
    to catch raindrops in pails
    and peek at the snails
    who
        s l o w l y
    crawl along the wet ground,
    moving their homes
    without making a sound.

Pigeons are so lucky;
    They are at that.
For when it rains, they play outdoors
    Without umbrella, boots, or hat.

They don't mind the raindrops
    They just peck and play for hours.
Pigeons are *so* lucky.
    Why don't people play in showers?

Monday/Muggy-day
Tuesday/Tornado-day
Wednesday/Windy-day
Thursday/Thunder-day
Friday/Foggy-day
Saturday/Soggy-day

Sunday
        At last!
SUN
        day.

SUNNY DAYS

Mile-long skyscrapers are my trees.
The subway's *whoosh*, my summer-breeze.

The hydrant is my swimming pool
Where all my friends keep real cool.

The city is the place to be.
The city is the place for me.

No matter
how hot-burning
it is
outside

when

you peel a
long, fat cucumber

or

cut deep into
a fresh, ripe watermelon

you can
feel
coolness
come into your hands.

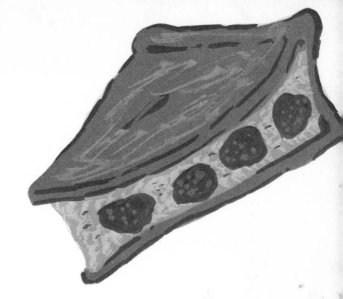

GREEN

Green sky.
Green kitten.
Green pie.
Green mitten.

Green here.
Green there.
Green, green everywhere!

But . . . Ha! Ha!

The color green quickly passes
When I take off
My green sunglasses.

TWO FISHY STORIES

1

jelly-fish
jelly-fish
I wish
you never
get spread
on my bread

2

I wish
the fish
wouldn't
swish
'cause then
I could
snatch
and
catch them

THIS TOOTH

I jiggled it
      jaggled it
      jerked it.

I pushed
      and pulled
      and poked it.

But—

As soon as I stopped, and left it alone,
This tooth came out on its very own!

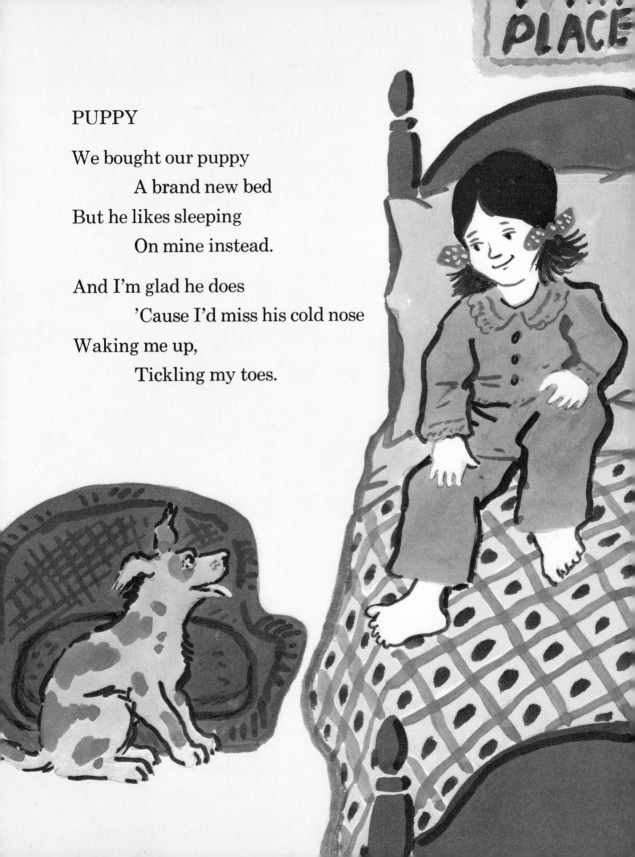

PUPPY

We bought our puppy
    A brand new bed
But he likes sleeping
    On mine instead.

And I'm glad he does
    'Cause I'd miss his cold nose
Waking me up,
    Tickling my toes.

NIGHTTIME

How do dreams know
    just when to creep

Into my head
    when I fall off to sleep?

ABOUT THE AUTHOR

Lee Bennett Hopkins, a former teacher and consultant with the Bank Street College of Education, is currently curriculum and editorial specialist for Scholastic, Inc. His work takes him on lecture tours throughout the country. Mr. Hopkins has edited several anthologies of poetry, both for children and for young adults, and is the author of *Charlie's World: A Book of Poems* and *More Books by More People: Interviews with 65 Authors of Books for Children.*

ABOUT THE ARTIST

Lawrence Di Fiori has illustrated many books for young people, one of which, *Antonio's Pizza Shop*, he authored. Mr. Di Fiori, whose work has been exhibited at the Philadelphia Museum of Art and elsewhere, is a winner of the 1972 PIA Graphic Arts Award for his illustration of *Cat O' Nine Tales* by Louis Untermeyer. He presently lives in New York City with his artist wife, Mila Lazarevich.

ABOUT THE BOOK

The art for this book was done in pencil and gouache and separated into two colors by the artist. The text was set in Century Expanded and the book was printed by offset.